A Woman's Survival:

Surviving the Military

by

Betty May

DORRANCE PUBLISHING CO
EST. 1920
PITTSBURGH, PENNSYLVANIA 15238

Dorrance Publishing Co
585 Alpha Drive
Pittsburgh, PA 15238
Visit our website at www.dorrancebookstore.com

ISBN: 979-8-8860-4388-4
eISBN: 979-8-8860-4480-5

This is a narrative that I am willingly sharing with all who choose to read it. I must warn you all that this is a graphic narrative that includes explicit sexual content, deception, human trafficking, racism, and lost lives. It will offend some; but these days, everything offends someone. This is based off of true events.

This book is dedicated to my parents, children, and all those who stood by me through my horrific encounters. Always remember your worth. Stay true to yourselves. The way people treat you is just a reflection of their own inner selves.

Hope is like the stars; they are always there, but the city lights dull the luminescence. Eventually, the luminous light is revealed once more. Remember we are all stars, dim at times but even the dullest light shines in the dark. Shine on with pure goodness and light, and let that light radiate through you always.

Chapter One

Betty and William Farris were married young. William, being more of the partying type, was an extrovert if you will. Betty was more conservative. Staying home and enjoying her own company and William's company was more her speed. William didn't seem to mind this. He used to joke that he always knew how true Betty would be to him, unless there was a single man at the grocery store. (I did all the grocery shopping.)

William and Betty would go out together from time to time if they weren't working . They made time for a date night here and there. William, when it was his turn to set up the date, always took Betty to some sort of dance club that was overfilled with druggies everywhere. Betty, trying to keep her husband happy, would accompany him with great protest to these sleazy establishments. She even went with him to the "gentlemen's club" and make her sit through a lap dance.

William and Betty would go together and drink a few beers and I (Betty) would try and make the best of it. I would ask William to dance with me, seeing how it would be a fitting activity for where we were. However, William would be more interested in drinking beer after beer after beer and having mindless conversations with anyone who would listen.

I, Betty, would set up dates like staying home and playing horseshoes, making bets of a sexual nature on who will win. We would be having dinner and cocktails, all ready to go, and having a great time out back throwing the horseshoes around. With protest, William would eventually come for my dates, even though dinner would be cold, and the sun would be setting, ensuring not more than one game of shoes could be played. His excuses were predictable. "The traffic was slow moving, babe." Or he would say, "At the last minute, the boss said I had to stay two hours over."

Whatever, we all know what excuses are…A butthole, everyone has one and they all stink! Betty would tell him that each time he gave her one. The two of them would laugh over how stupid the saying sounded. Through the laughter, Betty really was displeased with his bullshit. With her dazzling mouth of fully white teeth smiling and her steel blue eyes looking at you, it made it nearly impossible to know when Betty was upset.

William called it a pathetic resting bitch face. Betty kept mostly everything in. She believed that no one, regardless of if they listened or not, really did give a shit. So, she mastered bottling up her feelings.

Her biological father had screamed at her since she was a toddler, telling her tears and pathetic looks are just a woman's way to try and get what they want. He also told her that the only thing in life a woman is good for is her vagina. The voice inside Betty's head would nag that thought for a haunting number of years. Sometimes she was impetuous, to say the least Sometimes, her stoic ability would break, relinquishing quite the horrendous verbal diarrhea.

Be cautions of what you say to your children or other's children. You may think it will not linger with them into adult hood, but it does, and eventually, it can teach them to accept abusive behaviors. You are their inner voice.

Even with their personalities completely different, betty and William stayed married for eight years in the making. The two of them had three children together. Their names were Bean, Isaiah, and Adrey.

Chapter Two

Betty believed she was doing the right thing by her family by going into the military. She wanted to ensure that humanity would still be around when her children become adults. Plus, William was too fearful to join himself. Betty wanted desperately for her husband to join instead of her. Her attempts failed to sway him into joining. It was up to Betty.

Betty said, "I should be the one to stay home with the children."

William mocked, "All you women wanted equal rights, well, here you go. Betty, you are a woman, they would never put women on the front lines. You have NOTHING to fear. Besides, if I were to join, they surely will put me on the front lines. Do you really want to jeopardize my life over your idea? If you or I go, we could help humanity? Geez Betty, try to be practical."

"Yes William! I think it will help!" After her anger from his condescending words had subsided, common sense entered her head. William had a point, she thought. If I go and something happens, like I die, William would be able to hold down his one and only job to provide for our children. He tells me, "I make more than you, so I'm worth more alive than you."

William just laughs and walks away, mumbling… "My wife, the next GI Jane. Oh, Betty you have the most comically amusing ideas, too bad you won't follow through," William tauntingly said, doubting her ability.

"At least I have the courage to try." These two have a strange relationship. It looks like the perfect marriage with typical marital problems. Nothing seems too serious when viewing them from a fishbowl perspective.

Chapter Three

Off to the recruiting office Betty and William went. OS 1 Rett was a handsome, smooth-talking, muscular, dark-complexioned man. Everything that came out of his mouth validated my ideations, and I was sold. I think military men and women are the noblest and bravest. I, too, was going to be one of those women.

I signed into oath. I now belong to the government. William was giving me so much slack about it that he did not believe that I would actually go through with it. I laughed at his astonishment.

Back at home, William is in the back den, the children are at the grandparents' house, and Betty is in the bedroom when she hears William yell, "Betty, come here."

"I'll be right there," she yelled back.

He continues, "We need to talk."

Betty walked into the back den where William was. He immediately starting shit talking without even looking up. "Really, Betty, what are you going to do in the military? Are you really going to be able to handle seeing dead bodies? They don't put makeup on the dead ones, you don't have what…" He finally looked at Betty and saw she was standing there in her black lace bodysuit with her nipples peeking through, along with a seductive smile on her face.

"What are you mumbling about, William?" Betty walked closer to him and straddled his lap, lowering herself down onto him. She could feel the bulge in his boxers harden and become erect. William began again to speak, but Betty kissed his bottom lip, sucking it gently with hers. William's excitement took over, and he had given up on trying to talk.

The only thing now he could possibly get out was the seductive moan of pleasure. Betty pulled herself back and forth on him. William wrapped his arms around her waist, pulling her down into his hard lap repeatedly. Betty became moist with equal amounts of pleasure to William. The two of them lock this intense eye lock without skipping a single thrust. Betty pulled the black lace shoulder straps off one arm at a time, baring her hardened pink nipples that were filled with excitement. The sweat started to run down her breasts and just gave it the right chill to keep those pretty pink nipples just as rock hard as William.

William's tongue encircled her areola as he cupped her supple breasts in his hand. Circling around, pushing more intensely with each lick, causing Betty not only to become moist, but now also for her vagina to begin to throb for him to enter her. (Even though they were grinding each other, William has not yet fully been invited in her.)

"Suck on my nipples, and gently run and clasp them," she moaned. Provocatively, Betty slid the head of his penis on the outside of her, letting him feel the moisture he caused.

William whispered to Betty; "My cock is so hard; I want to be inside of you." Betty took William halfway into her, then pulled herself almost off, just to the tip of his penis. Then, she started sliding slowly down the shaft of him a little deeper each time, sending sensations all over their bodies. His face was going back and forth between both of her hard, pink nipples. sucking, licking, and arousing her. Her hands were running through his hair, enticing him further...

William had stopped his mumblings about what she could and could not do. The next morning, Betty was up and ready to go. The usual breakfast was on the table: orange juice, turkey bacon, pancakes, berries, and a side of coffee.

"Do you still want to talk about something, William?" He couldn't remember what he had wanted to say. (That is actually why I seduced him: so he would forget. I did not want to listen to any more of his condescending comments.) It worked like a charm. I benefited multiple times.

Chapter Four

I will join to ensure the country is still here for our children Bean, Isaiah and Adrey, along with anyone else's children that need protection. I really wanted for my husband to step up and say, "I don't think so; I will go. War is no place for my woman!" Oh no, he did not say that.

"Betty, sure, go ahead and I will stay home and raise the children." Oh shit, that was not what I wanted to hear.

Being the brave woman I am, I replied with, "Of course I will go, I want to." I was off to my parent's house to tell them what I had signed. This did not go over to well.

"What are you going to tell the terrorists, please wait don't shoot, but could you kill this spider?" They all laughed at that, like that would ever happen. They all mocked me. I sat there and thought, is that all I am good for, a pretty face, a babymaker? I'll show you all and myself, I'm going to be the best sailor I can! God bless America! I can do this!

My family kept saying things like, "You won't make it, please back out, you cannot do this. You are not strong enough to make it. Please do not go. Your children need you." Of course, they need me, that's why I am doing this, for them! Ugh. There was no belief in me. I believe that a man's life is not any less valuable than a woman's. We need both men and women to make the world run.

William was telling me before I left that he didn't want me to go, but he himself would not go because of the fear he possessed inside himself. He was afraid that if he went, he would be sure to be put on the front lines immediately, and he was afraid to die.

At the same time, I figured if I did die while fighting in the war, our children would be taken care of. Their father would still be home with them. Maybe that makes him stronger than me: being able to support children who lost a parent.

My father and mother, Joe and Maria, always told me how beautiful I am. They could not be prouder of what I am going to do, even though it breaks their hearts to see me go. They know I do not have what it takes, or so they think. My father is a Vietnam Veteran. I just want to make them proud. I am so much more than a pretty, baby-making vessel.

My father tells me, "Betty when you leave, those petty officers are going to be yelling in your face and you are unable to yell back at them. Well, you can, but they are going to inflict laborious work on you, like making you clean toilets with a toothbrush. You are going to have to touch spiders with your bare hands, not with shop vacs."

"Oh Dad, that's not how it is anymore."

"They tell you, Betty, when you can go to the bathroom and who you can be friends with, and they tell you not to wear makeup!"

"Come on, it can't be that bad, the recruiter did not mention anything like that."

Joe and Maria always raised me to tell the truth, even if it pissed people off, because they would respect you more for telling the truth after their emotions were under control. Therefore, I believed naively that everyone told the truth, even my recruiter. There they go again trying to get me to back out.

How silly, my recruiter would not lie; he was a first-class petty officer, he has integrity and honor. Look at him, his uniform is perfect, and his hair is also perfect. Here was this man that defended our country, and there is no way he would lie. The military does not produce liars. "Your recruiter is just telling you whatever you need to hear." No, it was just my family thinking that I was just too dainty to go fight the war on terrorism. They had no belief in me!

Chapter Five

I should have known that the recruiter was working on some kind of commission. I was supposed to be able to run over a mile in less than a certain time and do so many pushups and sit-ups. OS1 Rett had me demonstrate my physical abilities. or I should say, lack of abilities. As the recruiter, he was to be working out with me daily before I was sent off to the bootcamp. We only did that once.

I had most of it down, I was lean because that's the body I was given, a size two even after three children. Oh yeah! I was mean when people were wrong, and I had to voice my opinions to them so they can they know their wrongs and correct themselves. Fighting machine? With my mouth maybe, but I was never physically assertive.

That is why OS1 Rett was to be working out with me before leaving. He told me, "Don't worry, girl, at bootcamp, they will get you to the physical strength you need to be at. They will enjoy that spicy attitude of yours. It will help fend off the bad guys."

That right there should have been my red flag, but no, the spicy girl I am let it go to my head. When do I leave? Without any exaggerating, I left four days later for bootcamp. I went home and put my affairs in order.

Chapter Six

William did tell me that he was worried that the men in the military and all the dykes (as he put it) were going to take one look at me and try to take me away. I would just laugh because I was happy with him. "Let them try," I told him. "We've been together over eight years, and trust me people have tried, but I stay faithful to you."

God designed us two beautiful eyes to look at beautiful things, but then remember, he gave us free will as well to make the right choices. I choose to stay faithful to the one who does right by me, and the fact I don't want crotch crickets. (Did I mention I went to nursing school?) Sexually transmitted diseases are no joke. I want to keep myself disease free.

Chapter Seven

I'm being told to hurry up and say goodbyes to my family by some officer. I don't think so. There I go, telling her no ma'am, you wait on me. I may never see them again. I will take my time saying goodbye to them. (It was the last time that we would be that family standing there.)

If looks could kill, she and I would have both shot each other with our deadly looks. No matter what looks she made my way, I took the time I needed to say goodbye to my parents, William, and children. I had to leave a lasting impression on my children.

"I love you, and no matter what, I pray you take care of our children. Raise them right in the eyes of the Lord." Tears rolled down my face as I looked into his eyes.

He kissed my mouth and said, "I will always take care of them, Betty. They are the best part of us."

Maria just kept saying, "Don't go Betty, it's a mistake, William, stop her!"

Joe said, "Betty, you are an individual; stand out and stand above the rest. God is always with you. Remember people can only temporarily hold you down, but they never can and never will hold you down permanently!"

Bean told me, "Mommy, I am so proud of you, don't let anyone see you cry. You are my hero. I know how strong you are."

Isaiah said, "Mother, if I was bigger, I would go fight the terrorists, so you don't have to."

My Adrey, too young to talk at the time, just clung to me and literally had to be pulled off. The sounds of a child's cries are something that will scar anyone with a soul. It is a sound a mother will never forgive herself for, a sound I will never be unable to stop hearing, over and over in my mind.

I boarded the bus as my family and all the other families there stood by to see us off. Tears were falling from everyone's face. All the brave warriors on board the bus were holding back the tears, trying to be brave as we all saluted our families, assuring them we will return safe and sound like nothing has changed. Ah, yeah right. The strongest of men and women will be changed, no matter how strong they are. The effects of war change everyone!

Some changes positively and others negatively. Like Joe said, "You are an individual, stand above, and go beyond." All of us will be affected differently because we are all individuals. This bus has been driving for hours on hours. I sit there and think to myself, are we ever going to come to a stop?

I must have dozed off; I was startled when the brakes came to a screaming halt. I barely opened my eyes when the sound of a really angry, vertically-challenged man with a shrill voice said, "Get the fuck off the bus, move your ass now, you piece of shit, now, now, now!" (Wow, this guy appeared like he hadn't been laid in so long, someone needs to tell him about self-releasing.) I giggled a little over my own thoughts; big mistake that was.

"What the fuuuuck are you laughing at, you little fucking princess?" he asked me.

I went to reply, "Well…"

"Don't talk to me, you princess!" he screamed half an inch from my right ear.

I answered. "Sir, I have to talk to explain the answer to the questions you are asking." He started to get even louder, if you can find that possible. I shut up for the moment, but as soon as his spit stopped, he was hitting me in the ear, and I only heard ringing. I said, "Don't ask me a question if you don't want an answer! Sir!"

That right there was the start of a downward spiral. I was and never will be one to stand by idly when someone is wrong. I am compelled (almost by a compulsion) by some supernatural force to correct people who are wrong or at least to let someone know when they are wrong. We all need the opportunity to correct our wrongs. This is not the case in the military.

"Move, move, move," he commanded!

So, I did what any normal person would do; I shrugged my shoulders and said, "Move where," looking dumbfounded. I suppose it was a bit sarcastic, but really, where did he want me to move to? I ended up walking in a large gymnasium space repeatedly for hours, not just one or two, but four hours of just walking the gymnasium! Ugh.

I don't know how the hell this is supposed to be teaching me to fight off terrorists. Or even what I was supposed to be gaining from this, other than more of a sarcastic attitude. My thoughts were running through my mind. Make me walk aimlessly, you are not going to break me, you are just helping me. Each stride I took, I could feel my ass getting tighter and tighter. Free workout, I kept telling myself, no members fee, just pure, old-fashioned exercise. The entire time my spirits are high, no one can break me! (So, I thought at that time.)

The weeks are going by like molasses. None of us are able to freely call our loved ones. Some of the people were weak and didn't even make it over the passing weeks. They were dropping out like flies. I was dominating with a righteous attitude. They are weak-minded people, I assumed of those who had dropped out. How rude of me.

At this time, I did not realize that complacency was deadly. nor did I realize that complacency was just a noun for contentment. It took my great destruction and loss before I had my epiphany. It is so devasting that I had to endure such devastations before I realized what was being told to me on a daily basis for my entire life, all because of a pure, self-ignorant attitude I possessed.

Chapter Eight

The chief that was in charge of the division I was put in was another vertically-challenged man. What is it with short man syndrome, they really hate me? Or maybe they just hate that I can high dust and they cannot (lol). Back to the point. Chief Shorty was indeed handsome, he was just lacking height. He called me Smiley from the get-go. No harm in that, yeah right. Do not forget I am supposed to be a fighting, terrorist-killing machine! I am not supposed to smile.

We had road guards. Usually, the end of the line people did this job because they were the tallest of us all. The guard moves with a purpose to the front of the line to halt the vehicles, so the rest of the division does not get run over. This makes perfect sense. Chief Shorty apparently lost his senses when it came to me. He was out to break me. I'm at the front of the line, I stand at five foot two inches, one hundred and two pounds. That is with my boots on! I don't think the hum vees will see me. God, I hope they do.

"Airmen Smiley, you are now road guard, move your ass!"

I replied with "Aye, aye sir." This is my equal opportunity; I can halt traffic. The fact that I can see just slightly over the hood will not deter me. I flashed the biggest smile because, oh shit I think my life is about to end, each time one of these hmm vees rolls up on me. I am quite scared). And I bellow out, "Halt!"

I don't argue with him, each time he tells me to move my ass road guard, I do, and I do it with a purpose, too. Looks are deceiving, my tiny ass did manage to direct traffic without any accidental run downs.

"Smiley! Wipe that shit-eating grin off your face now before I come over there and wipe it off." Now, you would think Chief Shorty would have been smarter than me; one, he was older, and we are supposed to get wiser with age. Two, he made it up the ranks to chief. I am just a mere airman. Well, no, he wasn't in these aspects. He just kept elevating his blood pressure, constantly putting me as road guard, always trying to get me to wipe away my smile. Chief, let's get real, I'm going to do whatever is necessary to stop these vehicles, because the vehicles will do more damage to me and the rest of our division then we'll do to the vehicle. Duh.

The rage the penetrated right through me through his eyes when I had my oops of verbal diarrhea. Oh shit, how do I take that back? Since they are not supposed to lay hands on you, he punished me in several different ways. Chief Shorty was going to break me over that slip.

Now, back in the training center; "Smiley! Front and center!" Not in front of just the other female division, but the male division as well. I was front and center with all eyes on me, casting their ridiculous looks. No worries, this won't break me, no one here is Jesus, I kept telling myself. No one can judge me. Go ahead, get your entertainment that you guys all need. I stood at attention and took the public humiliation that Chief Shorty had to dish my way. Bring it on, it probably makes him feel taller was my thought.

Shit; a giggle slipped out. "Airman, you find me funny?" This was a rhetorical question, but I'm a wise guy.

"No chief, I just laugh when under pressure."

"Oh, we have a wise guy, do we?" Chief Shorty went and grabbed another chief, Chief Carroty.

This woman with a short butch haircut, red hair came, along with a first-class petty officer named Officer Homgal. Officer Homgal had dark hair, hair pulled tightly back in the neatest of buns, and she was built like a brick house. She came to join chief Shorty. There they were a power triangle around me. I'm going to get it now, I thought, and my smile faded quickly.

I had both women on either side of me, one in each ear, just barking orders at me. Let's not forget Chief Shorty, too. He was standing at the back of my neck with orders. I didn't know which one to listen to. I was doing jumping jacks, burpees, pushups; you name it, I was doing it. I think at one time, I was just jumping up and down, because I couldn't follow all the orders. Yes, I vomited. I ran to the trash bin and vomited. That still didn't stop the dynamic threesome. They just followed me to the bin and continued with their orders.

Back to front and center. I can't breathe. An order came for me to drop and do sit ups. I hit the deck, and still, I can't breathe. More orders. "Do the fucking sit ups now, Smiley!" "Kiss your knees." (It's been over an hour now.) Now they're being funny, there was no way I could do one more single sit up.

"Chief Carroty, hold my feet for me!"

Carroty is screaming, "You are so pathetic, what the fuck are you doing?" Laying on my back with just my knees bent, I couldn't move an inch, but I thought she could help me.

Homgal and Shorty are both screaming.

"No one is holding your stinky-ass feet. We don't want to be near your smelly ass!" Yet, they kept that tight triangle around me.

I mustered the strength to yell, "One team, one fight, get on those feet." Everyone person there started to crack up. Carroty turned as red faced as her hair. That was the end of my physical humiliation session. Finally, an order came from who the hell knows. They were all barking them at once. "Take your pathetic ass and go hydrate."

I'm thankful that's over, I couldn't take another minute. I hurt all over. But you guessed it, I still had a smile on my face. I exhaustedly made it to the head to hydrate. I was in for some serious delayed onset muscle pains.

When will they learn that I am not a horse? I cannot be broken. I learned how to bite the inside of my cheeks slightly to hold myself from smiling. Those D.O.M.S lasted for days.

Chief Shorty stopped having me be road guard after a few more weeks of him getting frustrated with my half grin. He and I had moved on to him looking at me and seeing me attempt to hold my smile back to him now thinking I just look foolish. It was impossible; nothing satisfied him. His look says it all. (I'm grateful he has self-control; those glares are so intimidating.)

Chief Shorty was actually smarter than me. He could physically assault me without even touching me. (Me and my fucking smile.) I ended up in the infirmary with a lifetime of arthritis. During one of our march sessions, we are to stay within the same uniformed step. If a person gets out of step, it screws up the entire division.

Normally, we were all good with staying uniform. We did a lot of marching. One particular session, as I mention, Chief Shorty kept having us do side pivots, trying to throw us off. A few times, we would get out of step on this. He was calling them as if it were a game of red light, green light.

Chief Shorty saw that it was messing with us and did it more. "The next person who takes a wrong step, I want you to kick them in the foot as hard as you can. Do not let one person mess up your stride." Ouch! It happened. I was out of step and this mother kicked me so hard, my calcaneus (heel bone) cracked right up to the top! The pain instantly kicked in; it was worse than when I gave birth naturally without any anesthesia.

I took that pain, because there is no way this half pint little prick chief will get the satisfaction of me falling out. I don't think so. I kept on marching the best I could, I couldn't bear weight on my left heel. Tears were streaming down my face with each step. Not a sound came from my mouth.

Chief Shorty asked, "Smiley, are you okay?"

"Yes, chief," I say. My eyeballs are sweating, but I am still smiling. He continued marching us. I spoke loud enough only for the piece of shit, no brained droid behind me to hear.

"You're a dumb droid. What the hell is the matter with you? You should grow a pair and known not to have done that, you easily-controlled pussy!"

Kick master sailor here didn't have anything other than, "Ahh, you were out of step, he told me to kick you."

"Smiley, fallout," he commanded. I did, and he wanted one on one with me. "What's wrong with you, do you need to go to medical?"

"No, Chief, like I told you, I can handle anything you can dish out to me, sweaty eyeballs and all."

I don't know why he ordered me to go to medical. He created this, so he should have to deal with seeing me hurt. I tried to argue with him that I did not need to go to medical, I could take it, I was just as tough as everyone else here. But I couldn't. I needed medical attention, so with the next order given for me to go, I replied "Aye, aye, sir."

X-rays taken proved my left calcaneus was in fact broken. It was a clear as day, no mistaking this one. This oversized doctor offered me morphine for the pain. What!? I cannot believe he just offered that to me. Hello, that is what you give dying people. I'm not dying, I just need a cast, which they do not do for the heel. Instead, they wrapped and air cast it and put me on light duty for several weeks. Because I denied the morphine, he gave me Motrin; he had said, "Since the pain doesn't require morphine, you'll be fine with these."

Because of this one injury, I had to extend my stay at boot-camp the additional weeks it took me to heal and then I had to perform the requirements to pass. I was pulled from Chief Shorty's division and now replaced into Chief Carroty's division. This meant even longer until I was able to see my children. A few weeks left again until I was done with camp. I'm still smiling when I feel the urge to, it's my right and no one will ever take that from me.

Chapter Nine

One day, Chief Shorty walked by the new division I was in and had some words with Petty Officer Homgal. I don't want to assume he was out to get me, but after they had their little discussion, she was riding me so hard about every little thing. Then, another time in front of the entire division, Petty Officer Homgal kept asking me question after question and would not let me have a chance to answer in a complete sentence.

I was getting angry, and we all know that I smile under pressure. Chief Shorty walked in and was barking at me again. (I think he secretly missed me and just was giving it to me while he could.) "Wipe that smile from your face, Smiley, I'm not here for your amusement, am I?" He walked away before I could answer and along came over Petty Officer Homgal and got right in my face, literally. When she spoke, her top lip was touching mine, but I still stood at attention. "Airmen Farris, shut your cocksucker!"

What? I didn't even say anything. I was not insulted in the least, that was the crudest but funniest thing anyone had ever referred to my mouth as. I laughed out loud right where I stood. I had a smile on my face so big it hurt. My reaction had her and everyone else laughing out loud. Chief Shorty comes flying into the room. "Smiley what the fuck is so amusing now?" This was it; I had had it with him.

I replied, "Chief, I was just told to shut my cocksucker by Petty Officer Homgal." I was still laughing and crying, I found it so crude but couldn't not laugh at it. It was hilarious, yet humiliating and degrading.

He looked right at me and started laughing, too. "I'm glad you have such an amazing sense of humor, don't lose that." I completed boot camp the next day. I was then sent to my school of training and that was a complete six-week joke. I learned nothing that could prepare me for what I was in store for. I was sent to a carrier.

"Fuck yeah," I thought. "I made it! How is that for my princess ass?"

Chapter Ten

I arrive on this massive ship; it's not a boat it's a ship, there is no mistaking it. I was so overwhelmed, but no one will ever see my fear. I was proud, brave, and ready. "Farris, reporting for duty, sir."

"Farris, its 0200. I'll show you to your birthing and you can find a rack, we will go over everything tomorrow at 0900. I'll send someone for you."

Below deck in the birthing are, I was given a dirty rack and told, "Sorry, there are no blankets left, deal with it." That sucked, but okay I dealt with it for a night, which turned into three nights without blankets or sheets. How fucking gross. The past three days, I would adventure out and try to find my way around the ship, seeing how no one cared to tell me where to meet at 0900 nor did anyone come and get me.

I was hungry and cold and wanted clean bedding. I ended up getting lost; when I would find my way into a space, someone would take me right back to the fucking birthing. Now could someone please take me to the galley? I could use something to eat. No, they act as if it was too much trouble. "No sorry. Ask someone else. You are not in my division."

Finally, I ran into someone that I knew from A-school, and they showed me where to go and get something to eat.

I was, after three days, led to my department where I would be placed; Air Del, V-1. I was now an undesignated airman, okay a fancy way of saying the Navy's bitch. I wasn't allowed to work as corpsman, seeing how they had too many females they closed it to us and only were only allowing men. I was made to work on the flight deck!

Petty Officer Ohla was the one who lead me to the "fly hole," A space where fly3 would meet every day, and that is where I was to report for working purposes. I was to be given a senior airmen or petty officer to show me the ropes. This was my first deployment and first time on a carrier as well.

Apparently, no one wanted to be bothered. Airmen Gerryus was a tall blonde woman; she must have been six two or more. She was put on the task of showing me around to get the required signatures I needed showing I have been shown around the ship. Gerryus took me to one space; I got one out of fifteen signatures. "Farris, I'll be right back, wait right here." So I did, and she never came back. I made my way to fly3 and just sat here until I was told what the next moves were. I quickly learned my way from fly3 to the birthing and to the galley. That is all I learned at this point. And already they are sending me up on the deck to chock and chain birds, whatever that means.

There was another petty officer in charge of training that was actually responsible for overseeing that this actually gets done before being allowed to work on the deck. The importance is no joke. When you don't know your way or what you are doing up there, it will cost you and/or your shipmates lives!

Her name was Petty Officer Lozano. (She had a strong resemblance to Chuck Norris.) She was Mexican-American, or at least, that is what she claimed herself to be. She was very efficient at her job. There were no missing signatures on anyone's form from this division. Somehow all the signatures I needed were there, yet I did not get them. I was told no that I only needed to get the one. I know she forged my initials and those other signatures that were needed.

As the weeks passed, I learned from repetition just what chocking and chaining a bird was now. It was terrifying to the core but I was helping keep America safe, and I made it. It became easier for me to move about the ship; I explored as best I was able. I ended up in some places I hope to never see again, like the weapons room. I'd rather stay on the flight deck, please.

I knew I had to find several ways from the birthing to the flight deck; my father told me that was the most important thing, always no matter what to know multiple ways to the flight deck. So, I did.

Things became routine, on deck all day, grab something to eat, back on deck. Laundry on Sundays. I was prohibited from going to the church-led services on board by my First-Class Petty Officer Ramus. He was very pleasing to the eyes, a smooth and handsome man. He always was around the master chief, and if he wasn't near him, he was playing guitar hero. He told me that I only wanted to go to church to get out of working on the deck because I couldn't handle it. This guy just shocked me. I couldn't believe one hour off the deck once a week was too much. Unbelievable. So church was quickly removed from me.

Chapter Eleven

Every morning, our captain, Captain Wheatfall, would address us at dawn. He would tell us, "Complacency will get you and everyone around you killed. Remember the dawn will rise each morning, and so will you if you do not fall into complacency." Then, he would send us off to our workstations.

I would report to work every day at 0600 with my uniform clean and inspection-ready. I was ready for work, squared away as we would say. I followed the rules because I could. I embraced the fact that I was a sailor. I was ready.

I recall distinctly when my LPO ABH1 Ramus called me out for my fingernails being too long. "Farris, what are the regulations of female fingernails?" The entire division was there; he was hoping I would not know and that mine were not in regulation.

"ABH1, they are to be no longer than the point of an ink pen tip." He proceeded to ask if mine were in proper regulation; so I did what anyone would do. I removed my ink pen and showed him that I was, in fact, within regulation. He did not have anything to ask me. I found it a sufficient way of telling him off.

Ramus had his wife and seven boys at home. He appeared to be a model sailor. He was a man that made his way up the ranks. Obviously, he could follow orders and do what was necessary to make it all the way from airmen to first class leading petty officer. At least, I thought so at the time.

He never saw or checked up on my work; he was always playing guitar hero with Master Chief Grandola. Ramus's lips were so firmly planted on Master Chief Grandola's butt. Like anyone else, Grandola didn't seem to mind his ego being stroked. He liked it so much he didn't seem to question the plethora of protein powder coming in and out of V-1.

I was being harassed by an airmen named Fronts; he constantly was hitting on me and never took no for an answer. He would tell me I was saying no but really my eyes were saying yes. Actually, my eyes said gross, I am repulsed by someone who says things like that. I put up with it because it was only air, and it did not really hurt me. He sat next to me a lot and put his arm on me. I would tell him, "Dude don't touch me, I don't like it." We had a safety zone, from your shoulder to your wrist was an appropriate zone. He seemed to miss a lot, he'd slip and cup my breast, still, I'd just punch him in the arm and tell him off. He really was an arrogant prick.

Fronts took it upon himself one day to try and use my mouth for fellatio; I don't think so! Wrong move! He pulled out this miniscule of a penis (in front of three other sailors) and waved it in my face saying; "Come on girl, you know you want this gold and diamond encrusted dick, give it a kiss." I kissed it all right, with my fist when I punched him right in the dick. How's that for a kiss? Then, I ran like hell. I told Ramus, and he launched an investigation immediately, no questions asked. (Front's is a tall, skinny white man that Ramus does not like).

The investigation was launched and proven that what I claimed was in fact true. Fronts was kicked out with a discharge other than honorable and flown off the ship. Now the gossip started; Farris is a man hater; she is here to get men thrown out. (Which couldn't be further from the truth. We need more men in society; these boys I have been encountering could use a good man for a role model.) I listened to the comments, but still, I held my head high. I knew the truth. It just became annoying that so many people on board could be so closed-minded.

Chapter Twelve

I worked on the flight deck, putting chains on the aircraft to ensure they do not go overboard. It was a super dangerous job. I did it with all one hundred pounds of me. I was so afraid the entire time I was doing it. Trust me, all of us up there were afraid, but that is what kept us safe and kept our heads on a swivel.

The bullshit nagging was starting to interfere with our safety. I just about went overboard twice. The first time, there were grease on the deck, and one of the aircrafts' exhausts was pointed at me. (That is some powerfully created wind.) I was literally being blown away. The grease slick wasn't helping any. Neither were the bunch of V1 guys standing there; they found it hilarious. "Look at her go."

They yelled out to me, "We'd help but don't want to be accused of sexual assault."

It was all good, I didn't go overboard, more like a body surf down the deck. This was an experience for me that no one can ever take. I just dropped to my knees and grabbed ahold of the safety handles. Then, I was assisted by real team players. The second time was comical, I will always look back on it and laugh. I think even the airmen who saved me will laugh, too.

It was once again on the flight deck, there was no apparent grease, only the strength and sounds of the exhausts. One craft turned, the exhaust was pointed in my direction, and there I go, weeeeeee, shit! This time, I'm running with it, trying to stop myself, but I could not stop! Oh shit, here comes the edge of the ship. My life starts to flash before my eyes. (It was darkness, no pictures of anything flying through my thoughts, just darkness.) "Oh Jesus," I prayed, when suddenly, Airman Wheatfull threw himself on me and tackled me!

"Thank you so much. I was about to go overboard. "I know," he replied, "I saw."

He piled me with seven chains to chain down the aircrafts with, and he stated, "Damn, Farris, you really need to hang onto like ten of these you are going to be blown away." I know it was a crack at my stature, but honestly, I did. Thanks.

Every day on deck wasn't this bad; it was better than up there at night. I was always trying to stay on top of my game, man this was intensely hard work. I loved every minute of it, because I was doing it. Yes, I was. I was supposed to work from 0600 until 2200, but it usually went over until 0230. I would sleep on breaks; if you get a half hour, you take it to sleep.

Most of the time I didn't like to eat on my breaks. One, I was exhausted, and two, I would have to bring the rest of the guys back food, because unfortunately some of the guys I encountered thought my place was in the kitchen. They can eat shit, and sometimes they would. I would say, "Yes, I'll go," to shut them up, but I did not always come back with trays for them. Oops did I forget? My silly lady brain couldn't remember what you men wanted from me. Oops.

I was made to work on the flight deck like I mentioned, but now they have me doing doubles: a full day's work and a full night's work. Whatever challenge there was, I did it. Now what do they think of me? I kept up with both the day and night crew.

There were some seamen that were machines. I don't how they did it but man I salute them. They know who they are. The ones with real honor, courage, and commitment.

Chapter Thirteen

Over the months of being on deployment, I saw for myself who were the lazy ones and who were the ones that busted their asses. After six months of being up on deck, I was pulled off. This was due to the fact that I was to wear glasses but never did and the training PO pulled me off decks. I was put in the kitchen, go figure.

There was this one first class that was to be leading us there, but her idea of leading and mine where so far from each other's. People ran all over her which was a shame because that's not how it should be. We have all heard the expression, "Shit rolls downhill," so guess what, I was one of the ones under her. Yes, that's right. I ate shit (figuratively) time and time again.

Every once in a while, though, I threw shit back without ever having to do anything but be me with my New Yorker, pricky attitude. I'm an individual. I will not be made to do something I don't want to, that isn't right.

I treated everyone with respect as long as they give it to me, but when they didn't respect me, watch out. My tongue was like a knife; it's my weapon. A voice is a powerful weapon when spoken with wisdom. (I was lacking wisdom and experience.) My voice was just a nag, but I didn't at this time know that. But everything happens for a reason.

The PO was giving me one hard time because everyone else basically told her to fuck off and disappeared. Well, I stood my post. There I was, and she was out to get blood.

"Farris! Swab the deck."

"Aye, aye PO."

"Farris! Clean the tables…clean the washrooms, dishes, redo the freezer!" Order after order came. She bellowed commands at me. I started at 0600 and it was now 1300.

I was hungry. I said, "PO, I will finish as soon as I take my lunch, I have to eat." She didn't like that at all.

This woman followed me all through the chow line and told me, "No, you will do what you are told now." Okay, that is what she thought. I continued to go through the line and get my food.

I figured she would have walked away by now; she was more persistent than me. Whatever, follow me, it's amusement for me, (right now). She followed me to the table and continued to tell me stop eating and finish doing what she told me to do. Ha, still I sat there and refused to stop; I still kept my mouth to a minimum. I would tell her, "Doesn't look like I'm moving, does it"?

Well, when she put her hands on my tray, that was it. I lost it. "What the hell, you dumb witch, you apparently get to eat, back the fuck off. I'm going to eat whether or not I have an order to or not! Go clean the deck yourself if it needs to be done so badly. You dummy! Now leave me alone for thirty minutes to eat!" Wow that felt good to say for a split moment.

I was loud, so loud that the lieutenant that was in one of

the spaces on the other side of the galley came out with quickness. "Shipmate, move your ass front and center!"

"Sir," I replied, ready to explain why I was so nasty; but before I could reply any more, he shut me down.

"Not you Farris, PO CS1, front and center." He chewed through her like a rat in an inflamed trash can on someone's stomach.

I just sat there eating my meal, thinking, yes! Justice is served. Then, this extremely tall, dark lieutenant came walking my way. Oh shit, here it comes, my turn.

"Farris, when you are done with chow, you have liberty (free time) until 0600 tomorrow. Awesome.

I just replied with, "Aye, aye, sir, thank you!" I did not rebut any words he said. I did see him later that night and he did tell me that my efforts did not go unnoticed by everyone, and that I should hang in there.

CS1 did not like that fact she was put in her place, but she was grown; she let that go the next day as if it were nothing. Now that's my kind of ship mate and leader. Don't hold it against us; we have more important things to worry about out at sea. She and I learned to deal with each other, which was great because I could be very difficult to deal with. Yes, even with my princess ass, I can be difficult.

Once she and I taught each other, she got a new boss named Senior Chief Mick. He was another vertically challenged man. I should have seen it; he and I were going to clash. I don't know what it is, but it is inevitable that short men and I clash. He used to ride my ass so much I swear it gave him a hard on with the sick pleasure he seemed to get from it.

Senior Chief Mick said, "Farris clean the refrigerators."

"Aye, aye Senior Chief."

I would do it and then he comes back and tells me," Looks like shit, you didn't do anything." What? Did he just question my integrity? I take pride in the fact I tell the truth.

"Senior Chief, I would not lie to you, you had better take a look at that because its clean." He and I would argue back and forth because I was telling the truth and he was an idiot. Really, I was. I would argue that I did it. I should have worked smarter and not harder. No, I was a big dummy, I had to work harder. Every time I'd argue, he didn't care, he would award me more orders to clean. I would clean things like the bulkheads for four hours straight; how flipping clean do bulkheads need to be? Apparently, until Senior Chief looked pretty in them. Shit, this was going to take all of my deployment.

A few weeks of me and my big dummy ass working harder, not smarter, went by. It's all good. I did it every day. Finally, though, another first class that would watch the amusement of me being a big dummy for the past few weeks came along who I talked with on a daily basis in the galley and in the smoke pit. He pointed out that I should just tell Senior Chief that I was on it, after he tells me to do it again. "I don't know about this, because I have integrity," I said.

"Yes, Farris, most of us do, but work smarter, not harder." Okay, let me try this.

Without fail, here comes Senior Chief Mick. "Farris, the refrigerators need to be cleaned; they look like shit."

"Aye, aye, Senior Chief. I'm on it." I moved over there, stood by the refrigerators, and stood some more. Ten minutes later, Senior Chief came back, looks at them and says…

"See Farris, if you just did it right the first time, you wouldn't have to redo them over and over again. It's called working smarter, not harder."

"Geez, Senior Chief, I apologize."

"It's never too late to correct your wrongs, Farris," Senior Chief Mick said and walked away. You have to be kidding me, I thought. There was no way I hid the expression of "you big dummy" on my face. I just looked at him.

The first class with the awesome advice said, "Good job Farris, I'll see you in the smoke pit."

Again, my theory of vertically challenged men I had encountered had been true to some degree. I really agitate them. I should go right for fluffing their egos. Nah, it's not my style. I'd rather hand them their asses when they are being buttheads. When will I learn?

Chapter Fourteen

Here I thought that the military was about honor, courage, and commitment. Well, it is; however, they cannot weed out all the shitbags, so they teach the ones who do possess honor, courage, and commitment to play the game with those that do not have these characteristics. This is because so many terrorists are already right here in America posing as patriotic Americans.

I have never been one to be racist. I believe everyone should be given the equal opportunity to prove whether or not they are respectful, regardless of the color of their skin. I would help anyone in need, regardless of the color of their skin. I, however, have been experiencing racism, known as "white privilege," here in the military, on a regular basis.

I live life by treating people the way I want to be treated. Maybe in a fictitious world that is true; however, in the military, it is not. You are made to feel what it is like to be "white privileged," as though I had a choice in the option of what color I was born. There are some nationalities that believe one color or the next has lesser value, and it is their mission to make sure they impose those views on you.

On board the carrier, you need a noise attenuating headset (which are double sealed to help reduce the noise from the aircrafts). Everyone is to be given a set. However, we're not all given what we are supposed to be given.

The people that I encountered while in the military were so racist toward me. I was not given my hearing protection because of the fact my skin is white. The people I dealt with were of Spanish descent and straight out told me, "You don't deserve to be protected, you were born with a silver spoon up your ass!"

This was all over my skin color or lack thereof. I believed that everyone here wanted to fight the war on terrorism and keep these cowards out of America. While enduring operation freedom, the ship was attacked with some sort of chemical warfare.

My true brothers and sisters went up on the flight deck and scrubbed it clean with me. The cowardly were below decks playing video games. We were given face masks to wear because of chemical warfare inventions. I was given a proper mask. However, I was given a broken air canister that provided the clean air to breathe. Unable to breathe without the air canister and lacking air, I took off the mask and dealt with the effects of whatever I was breathing in.

What was it I breathed in? After that, I was put on detail that kept me below decks. Still V1 but in training and supply. Petty Officers Lozano and Agular both ran this department under Ramus.

Chapter Fifteen

I was raped repeatedly by ABH1 Agular (piece of shit). He was of Spanish descent. He used to wait in the shadows of the night in the light lockers and wait for me. He would make it so I had to work late so he could get me. He was always threatening to throw me overboard if I didn't go along with it; in fear I would be thrown into the ocean, I let him have his way with me. There were several times I remember him hanging me over the side of the ship right under catapult three, telling me, "No one will hear you scream, if you keep trying to get away, I will drop you." I would just look down at the illuminating jelly fish with tears streaming down my face, praying to please let it be over soon. I was afraid to go to medical because of the connections he had there, and because I was embarrassed.

Agular had locked me in the sixth deck, which is a space located way below decks, and he would leave me there for twelve hours at a time. One of the times I was down there, he made me go onto the top level which you couldn't get up or down without a ladder. I went up with a ladder, but on the way down, he moved the ladder away. He left me stuck up there until I could not take it anymore. I had to come down. He said I could only come down if he assisted me down. I argued but I didn't win. I started to get down without his help anyway, I didn't care if I broke something, maybe the rapes would stop.

As I dangled there from the second level inside that space on the sixth deck, Agular ripped down my pants and performed UNWANTED cunnilingus. That's not even the worst part; I was on my period! So, my bloody sanitary napkin was all over his chin, I could never tell someone how disgusting that is. I am so ashamed. I was being held up by him with his arms around my hips holding me into his face. I was fighting and punching him so hard, trying to poke out his eyes when finally, he had enough and dropped me and said, "Clean up. All you white bitches taste the same."

The hatch slammed shut, and he dogged down all the locks and kept me in. Before he left, he did throw me cigarettes and a drink. Later, he came back and let me out. He told me if I was to mention anything, he would throw me overboard.

I went to Ramus because I will never be told not to tell! Ramus looked me square in the eye and, I quote, said, "Look at you Farris, what do you think is going to happen?" He then proceeded to tell me I was fabricating this because I could not hack the laborious work. Ramus and Agular are extremely tight friends; they are both Spanish. Ramus would not launch an investigation. Instead, he started to feed Master Chief Grandola with bullshit; I was a slacker, whore, troublemaker, a manipulative, dishonest shitbag.

I fought back a few times when there was no chance of me getting thrown overboard, but it never stopped him. If anything, it excited him. I tried everything I could to avoid him, but the Spanish men just wanted to stick together and say I was just a whore that wanted it and said I was trying to get men kicked out of the military. Those pieces of shit are not men; they are cowards. No means no. His mother really messed him up.

Agular used to drug me, too, and when I would go for a urine sweep, they would switch my urine to not set off alarms. Ramus and Agular would tell us where and how to cover the drugs in our systems. I made friends with Lozano, thinking there would be power in number;, however, that is where my great fall began…

With her, I was able to break away from ABH1 Agular. She protected me from him somehow. I think it was because she was extremely cunning and could manipulate people to do what she wanted, all without a single shred of guilt. She also had no remorse for anything. She bragged about her family having ties to the mob, and she showed me pictures of bodies without their heads and with all other limbs cut off and just the torsos left. She took pride in telling people her "family" did that. The psychological war she used was to be far more damaging than the rapes. After I had seen the pictures of this hacked up bodies, I was afraid of what she and her family were capable of. Lozano was bellicose by nature.

After the raping had stopped, it was a new ball game that I was in. I had been sucked into this tremendous drug-ring. She started showing up in the middle of the night to my rack to see how I was. It was a form of psychological war warfare I had not quite understood at this time. Here I thought she was truly looking out for my well-being, but no. It was indeed a form of terrorism I was oblivious to. Yes, right in our own military, terrorists are hard at work.

Did I mention she bragged about her "family" running a heroin ring? No wonder I ended up addicted to heroin. A few drops in my mouth while I'm asleep will surely get me hooked. I was being drugged right there in the military, secretly and unwillingly! Fucking cowards! The command sweeps are not enough to keep drugs out of the military. That is one thing I do not believe we will ever win: the war against drugs.

I let my husband know of the horrific nature of crimes being done, and he told me how all I did was whore myself out. What!? You've got to be kidding me, he really said that to me. Yet he was the one, my husband, that would tell me, "Hey you should take pictures of the hot lesbian that keeps coming to your rack, you know, some sex pictures." Perverted thought, which what guy isn't perverted? It is hot when two consenting women are having sex, and one of them is not your wife!

Now before any judgements are made let me just say; I called my husband for advice and instead got permission to do anything sexual with ABH3 Lozano. To me, that was the second time he, my husband, failed me. It wasn't sexual to me, it was what I thought of as protection. It later turned into a love, I guess. I was blinded to see that the addiction I had was because of her.

What kind of partner shares? Not me. If the tables would have been turned and William said to me, "Geez Betty, I think I need to get my rocks off because I want to see what it's like to be with another man," I would not have given permission.

His perverseness' backfired on him. We ended divorcing, and neither one of us have any respect for each other. He thinks I'm a whore, and I think he is a coward. In my personal opinion, anyone that shares an intimate bond with each other should hold onto it and cherish it always. I would never share my lover. Materials yes, lover no.

In a way, it was a blessing in disguise. I would come to discover this "blessing" much later. Lozano and I, the verbose pair we were, shared our animosities over William's willingness to share me. We also talked about how Ramus and Agular were no good shitbags in disguise.

I never did understand what a shitbag in disguise was until I experienced them firsthand. With the form of warfare she was using on me in pair with Ramus and Agular, Lozano and her "family" were the lesser of the evils.

Each night, she was coming to my rack and relentlessly gaining my trust. She was also ensuring my addiction. Still, I had not realized that she was the one drugging me. It was all warfare. They were the shitbags in disguise. The more she and I shared our thoughts, the more it brought forth this enormous-sized, ungracious obscurity I held inside toward men.

At the same time, our conversations brought us closer. The late-night rendezvous with a few drops here and a few drops there. It even went so far as having drops put in my cigarettes, so during the day I had some drugs in my system. She was the one that was able to disguise through me. Agular and Ramus's attempts had failed. Or did they? The raping and ridicules where all a part of the psychological warfare that was being done. My thinking was distorted, along with shame and guilt of the acts having been done, and I couldn't see the manipulation being done.

Lozano would tell me how when she was with people, they would never commit to her. She had this thing for married women. Of course, married women were not going to leave their husbands for her. She had a way with her words. I felt like all she needed was someone to be there for her. I was blinded by her lies and cunning ways. I have a God-fearing, God-loving soul that didn't want to believe the truth in those labels. I wanted to help her. I wanted to show her what I have inside of my soul: Jesus and love.

I was taught to share that goodness and that love with those in need. Lozano was definitely in need of being loved. She and I needed each other and our need/desire (addiction) for each other grew into this tremendous inclination that only she and I shared. It was probably the heroin she was dropping into my mouth in small doses at the time to keep me hooked, all while filling my head with her corrosive lies.

The other shipmates on board would tell me to stay away from her because she was no good. They said she was a homewrecking whore. I assumed it was all just gossip, seeing how I dealt with my own feelings of being a man hater.

Lozano was discharged from the military two years before I was supposed to be. She lived with me in an off-base apartment which I paid for, never asking her for rent money because of the fact she served in our country's military and was discharged from the military and still was not working yet. It was a difficult adjustment being in the military and then transitioning back to civilian life, which we are indoctrinated to believe that we are above the common civilians. I was going to be there for her to help her through this adjustment. I live my life with true, undeniable patriotism. I was going to stand by my war sister in her time of need. That is the patriotic thing to do. Or maybe it was again the heroin addiction.

With Lozano being gone, I was alone to contend with these issues onboard the ship, which I was handling. The weeks were going by, and I was reporting to work as I was expected to do. Lozano confided in me how the smuggling was being done. They were sending it in packages of "the protein" and in Visine bottles. I had a lot inside to deal with. Over the next five months, I drank myself into a drunken stupor. Jägermeister helped repress the daunting thoughts that filled my mind. Rapes, drug lords, my husband thinking I'm just a whore. I can still feel the penetration happening even though it's not happening. I drank more.

While on board the incubus I called home with just my thoughts tormenting my wellbeing and the gruesome things I witnessed as well as endured, I finally broke. They win. I cannot hold it together anymore. I tried to seek help but was denied. I lost myself, my worth, my freedom, my sanity. I became a prisoner of war without so much as being "held" captive.

The military is just a mafia that uses their foot soldiers as pawns; they have no remorse or regard for any of our lives. They are like any other militia group. What sets us apart from any other terrorist group? From basic training onward, we are taught to fight or flight, to obey, and to follow orders, no questions asked. I am definitely the kind of woman that needs to know why.

Chapter Sixteen

Myriads of military women and men are diagnosed with split personalities, bipolar disorder, narcissism, PTSD (post-traumatic stress disorder), and MST (military sexual trauma). War is an infinite battle that can never be completely wiped out, with the exception of wiping out the entire planet. With all the nuclear and mass destructive weapons hidden throughout our planet, that is most likely to be the expiration of humanity.

Other than honorable and dishonorable dischargers, medical discharges were bestowed upon many. This is the military's way to not have to provide any benefits, leaving so many to develop into drug and or alcoholic addicts. You gotta love the loop holes the government finds to get away with against the country's service men and women who fought and are fighting for the very country. It is appalling.

Military sexual trauma is a difficult one I have to cope with. It is an extremely difficult situation to prove. Personally, I find it the most devastating. I am not considered a valor, seeing how most rapes go unseen and/ or are swept under the rug. A countless number of men and women get raped, and they go unreported out of degradation.

I made it home in a physical sense, but a part of me was lost at sea that can never be revived. Not all injuries are visible to the eyes, and with that comes an avalanche effect of destructions. Stationed back on land and having finished my overseas tour, I was now having to finish my land base aspect of my tour. I came back the same Betty Farris, or so I had thought.

I didn't find being raped to be such a problem (at the time). I would never have thought something that was not in my control would or could ever be used against me. It can and it was used against me. It was the demise of this brave young mother who was fighting not only the war on terrorism, but the unspoken war of Americans against Americans.

I hadn't realized how much the rapes and the brutality were going to impact my life and the lives of my three small children, until I ended up in the psychiatric ward. Even still, the monumental effects didn't register with me until years later. Repression is no joke; it is the devil's recipe for a slow, hideous, drawn-out death. The military had diagnosed me. The officers are the ones who had come to their conclusions without any deliberations as to how their diagnoses were ultimately going to oppress and encumber my life.

At the evaluation, in walks this scrawny woman with thick, coke bottle glasses on. "Farris, follow me." She and I enter a room with a square, deep cherry wood colored table with six men sitting around it. "Farris sit here." Go figure; it was at the head of the table I was to sit. Fuck, I feel the intensity penetrating my resting bitch face.

The oldest looking man to my right was Doctor Dumas. He was the one who conveyed to me his opinions of what diagnosis I have. "Farris, you have a serious problem here, do you realize you need help?" he asked in a southern drawl.

I responded with, "Don't you think you all should introduce yourselves to me before I answer any questions?" There goes that southern drawl again.

"We are all doctors here, and we will be asking the questions. Now Farris, do you or do you not realize that you are mentally ill?"

What the fuck, mentally ill? Listen here you swinging, arrogant jerk, you need a review on what mental illness is! I was screaming this on the inside, but I just listened to what they all had to say. "Farris, answer the question. Are you or are you not aware you need help?"

"I apologize, I must have zoned out," I stated, rather disdained.

Good thing, too, if I would have said what I was thinking out loud, well, I would have proven them all correct. "No, I do not agree. I'm here because I chose to flee instead of fight."

"Do you find yourself to be normal?"

"Yes, of course I do. Well, normal for myself, but who's to say what normal is? I can't possibly please everyone, that is impossible." Doctor Dumas raised his pen and wrote who knows what down.

"Farris, do you know what the word narcissism means?"

"Yes, I do."

"Do you? Farris you are a narcissist."

"Okay doc, whatever you say." I impetuously answered all the questions that came flying out of their mouths. (One question they never asked was, "What happened?")

"I must ask you Farris, do you have trepidations?"

"No."

"Why not? I cannot predict the future, whatever happens will happen. I do not control the future. So, you think I was just speaking of your own future? Did you even consider that I was including someone else's future?"

"No. I don't control their futures and hello, I am the only one in the room that you all are trying to interrupt, so of course I think of myself; you phony fools! Besides, I don't worry about things that haven't taken place yet, it's a waste of my energy. I have no control over how anyone else lives their lives, nor do I worry about people I don't know."

"Why do you not care about other people?"

"I didn't say that! I said I do not worry about what goes on in other people's lives, I only worry about and am dedicated to my family and my life. I am empathic towards others' situations at times. Why are you trying to provoke me?"

"You think I am trying to provoke you, Farris? There is a long list of mental illnesses I have to award to you. However, I do not advise anymore for today. I will have the nurse bring you something to help you relax, this way you'll be able to tolerate further conversations without having so many anxieties."

"Let me get this right doctor Dumas, you are going to drug me, because I do not agree with your bullshit labels?"

"No, no Farris it's medication for your agitation and outbursts you clearly are having."

"Bullshit! You should be imprisoned for smuggling drugs!" Exasperated, Doctor Dumas diagnosed me as schizophrenic and bipolar with chronic depression and anxiety. There was nothing about PTSD or MST.

I unleashed anger. I had it under control but how could they not mention MST? Why wouldn't they ask me what happened or why I did what I did? You cannot just label me without getting to know me and asking the right questions. I mocked his accent, "I must drugggg yoooouuu for not obeyinggg." That was the end of my verbal diarrhea, thanks to the two muscular men. One held me still, the other injected me with…

"Put her in her bunk, she will be out for hours."

I woke up at 0500 still thinking it was the night before. I was ready to wage war with these foolish doctors. Yet something bizarre had happened; I was inert. I could hear the doctors and other people in the hallways. Panic had set in…Am I paralyzed, am I dead? As panicked as I was, I was able to interchange mentally with myself. I could be dead (remember that hearing is the last sense to go). Then why can I still see? I don't know exactly how long this went on, but I obviously wasn't dead.

The doctors enter my room. I was at this point able to sit up, wary of what was to come. "How are you feeling, Farris?"

Incoherently, and surprised I could speak, I replied, "I'm exhausted and I can't feel my body."

"That's because we had to medicate you last night, Farris, you were irate." I mumbled an apology. "Farris are you aware you are in need of help?"

"No, but if you want to give me help, I won't stop you." My speech was becoming more understandable. (Yet I was unable to get worked up, and I wanted to). "Hey, what is it I need help with again?" I asked.

"Farris, before we get into that, you need to take these."

"What are they?"

"Medications that will help relax you, please take them orally because the alternative route will be us giving them to you."

"I'll bite you." They all broke out in laughter.

"No, Farris, the cavity we will put them in doesn't have teeth." Their wittiness didn't amuse me.

"That is an exit only, give them to me." I swallowed all of them, not knowing what they were. I just didn't want the back door route with role-playing proctologists.

I'm confident my first constitutional right declares freedom of religion, speech, press, and assembly. Infringing on these is unconstitutional, except when it comes to the military personnel within this particular facility. Once you commit to the military, you are to become an android, perfunctorily letting go of your constitutional rights!

I look at the oblong yellow pill, it and had the number four hundred craved in it. The two other pills were round and yellow with WW277 craved into them. I thought, I've never seen pills like these. Those were Seroquel and Lithium Carbonate I had later come to find out. This was an extremely formidable amount of drugs to calm me when I wasn't in a psychotic state. Goddam the pushers!

Chapter Seventeen

Most evidence suggests that the saftest way to quit taking Lithium is gradually, over a period of weeks, as well as with the Seroquel. Abruptly stopping either medication can throw you into a spiraling psychotic state. In my case, it was not done in the professional, educated way. Over the next several weeks, I remained detained, having to take these pills that were making me ill.

The detainment was awful. I had watched six of my shipmates come into detainment. There was an obvious pattern here. Marge Schmelow was assigned the rack next to mine. There were two to a room. "Farris! You're here too, no one knew what happened to you. Are you alright, what happened, when did you get here, what did you do?"

Schmelow was unremitting. I was just grateful to have her there with me. Schmelow and I had become close while on the carrier together. So, I didn't let the annoyance of the babbling get to me. I just listened in bemusement, because of the pills they had given me. Schmelow and her incessant questions about me, along with all the details about what had taken place with her, well, the entire conversation seemed to have blended all together.

"Schmelow! Lock it up! Save some for the morning, my brain is literally throbbing from all of that. Let's get some sleep, maybe my subconscious can sort some of that out."

She and I both laughed over what I had just said. "Goodnight, Farris."

"Goodnight Schmelow."

"Farris, um, can I ask you a question?"

"No, go to sleep."

"I'm just messing with you, Farris." We snickered and finally fell asleep.

Zero five hundred, REVEILLE, REVEILLE came over head. "Farris you up?"

"Yes."

"Are you going to attend group?"

"No, Schmelow, I am not."

"Please, why not? Do it for me; I don't want to do it alone."

"You are a pain in the butt. They don't do anything in group but explain how society says we should react. It's not helpful," I told her.

"Betty, will you just go with me as my supporter? Betty?"

"Whoa you must truly want me there, you called me by my first name."

"Please Farris?"

"Ugh, yes, I will, but do you think we could get through breakfast first? It's too early to dive into a bunch of drug-pushing, closed-minded doctors that still believe in Sigmund Freud's theories. Come on, the man died in nineteen thirty-nine; I personally think his theories should have been buried with him. He believed we all have pent up desires to be incestuous."

"Farris, you're so crude."

"No, I'm not. I'm simply sharing the useless knowledge I learned in psychology class. Marge, come on, admit it, you want a brother daddy. What would the children call him? Uncle daddy?" I playfully teased Schmelow. She gave me a derisive laugh as we left the room for roll call and breakfast.

After breakfast, everyone there would take their pills, like good little androids, myself included. The newfound numbness I had developed from these pills transformed me into the android that the staff had desired. They could have told me that my legs needed amputation, but my drug induced psychosis had me remiss.

Therapy sessions are a joke. A petty officer had us sit around an oblong grey and white speckled table. There were about twelve rolling chairs, which only six had been needed. The room didn't have one window. Along the dullest beige bulkheads and in the corners had piles of broken chairs, spider webs going up the bulkheads and spreading out in the corners. The room was ludicrous; I personally could not take anything being said in here seriously. I was too distracted with the lack of professional appearance.

In the middle of the bulkhead hung a white erase board, slightly leaning to the left. The petty officer wrote some bull up there. Coping methods: Exercising, deep breathing, yoga, meditation, and I forget what else. These so-called professionals are comical. Tell me, how should I deal with the brutal rapes that I endured? Nothing was mentioned about rapes or seeing chopped up bodies to help me cope. Just heavy-duty pills to keep me blank and silent. Remember to breathe.

I asked the petty officer a simple question. "What have you been through yourself to say these methods of coping actually help? Do you even know why just one of us, just one, are in thus ward?" Petty Officer Zuccarello demanded I get up and stand at attention. While he verbally assaulted me for asking what he actually knows.

After a few minutes of gibberish bouncing off my eardrums, it stopped. I stood there at attention and said, "You have made it perfectly clear you don't."

"Farris, I didn't make anything clear to anyone, I outrank you; I ask the questions around here! Is that understood?"

"I understand however, I do not agree, your logic is nonsense. Because you out rank me, you get to disrespect me? You are here to teach us coping methods. Here you are being ignorant to even suggest, let alone, say, I am not allowed to ask questions! Hello captain obvious, we are in a psych ward, it's supposed to be beneficial to the person admitted here, me! You should be asking questions and revealing whatever it was to have landed me here, so I can cope! Think outside the box."

From that moment on, Petty Officer Zuccarello did not hold a conversation with me, let alone did he make eye contact. Yet again, I thought silently in my head, he has proven he really is a "petty" officer. As for me, I was now considered hostile, which awarded me the right to two strip-searches a day instead of just one. Lucky me, I just have to grin and bear it. That is precisely what I did.

I exaggeratedly grinned and proudly (yet so very ashamed) bared it all every time. Using my defense mechanism, I sarcastically said, "Are you guys at least going to make it rain?" even though I was terribly uncomfortable revealing myself. I mean hey, come on, it isn't my choice to strip, it was an order, which is against my will, which was adding pressure and stress inside of me. This was a recipe for complete unbe-fucking-lieve-able, mayhem.

Yet, I was bestowed with the gift and curse of stoically accepting everything, even when and if I am falling apart. I am told at times (rare times) that it is a fantastic talent. Most times, people tell me it's my resting bitch face and my dark, malevolent eyes that do all the talking. Honestly, I think it's my lips that do all the talking, but I would never consider myself in any way to be malevolent. Oh no, there is that narcissism spewing out.

I learned to just nod my head and agree, regardless of how jacked up I thought it to be. They broke me. I personally took a vow to stay silent and stop eating. I was still taking the medications I was forced to take.

The silence did not impact anyone other than me. Not one of the staff asked me why I was silent. Not one the pathetic staff asked me why I was in here. I guess it must be outrageous to ask the question, "Why or did you threaten to hurt yourself?" Or, "Did you attempt to hurt yourself?" Those are the events that would land someone in a psychiatric ward. Clearly, it was beyond their scope of practice. Regardless of that, I was released from the psychiatric ward without one of them ever knowing what I had been through.

Chapter Eighteen

I was released back to the ship three days ago without being allowed to shower or change my clothes. I did not have Captains' mass either, trust me, I put in for it. Yet I was denied! The XO denied me, too. I couldn't even speak to the jag. No, I saw the CMC.

It was in the p-way with the hideous green tiles that were making me sick. The sight of them flashed images I had been desperately trying to forget. The thoughts literally sent me into a panic. I could feel my temperature increase along with my heartbeat, which felt like I was going to spit it right out of my mouth into the CMC's face if I tried to speak. I was purely petrified. This is one of the moments I find my resting bitch face to be a gift; I held that face without a break and without a tear.

"Farris, enter." As I entered the room handcuffed, I was told to take a seat. There were seven chairs around the rectangular table. CMC O'Doul sat at the head of the table; I sat to his left. There was another petty officer there who stood behind me. (He is the one with the key to the hand cuffs.)

I spoke first. "Sir…" I was abruptly interrupted by the CMC's booming voice.

"Farris! Lock it up and listen, goddammit!" I didn't even blink. "You are here by a disgrace to your entire command and your country! You are being discharged from the military. You are being reduced in rank before your release, you will receive no benefits or help from the military. Everything promised you can kiss goodbye, just like you can kiss your ass goodbye."

Impetuously, I slammed my handcuffed hands down on the table and in my calmest voice, I said assertedly, "Get on with it already." CMC O'Doul 's eyes widened to the point I thought they were about to fall out. His veins in his forehead and neck started to visibly throb. I didn't break eye contact once. The silent, thick tensions in the room were suffocating.

Instantly, he was eerily tranquil. His eyes and veins went back in place, and then this awful sinister of a smile spread across his face. "Farris, you are hereby released under other than honorable conditions with bad conduct. Now, get the fuck off my ship and off my naval yard."

All I could muster was, "Aye, aye, sir."

I walked out, still handcuffed and not appropriately dressed to go anywhere, let alone outside. I asked what happened to my clothes. They mysteriously disappeared. However, one of the shipmates gave me a pair of jeans two sizes too big and a tee shirt. They allowed me to change into those clothes before escorting me to the gate in the Portsmouth, Virginia shipyard, where I was released at 0200. I had no way but by foot to get anywhere.

My home state was only on the other side of the country, only two thousand, three hundred and twenty-six point four miles, give or take a few. I walked all the way to Norfolk to get to a bus station. I made it there in just about five or six hours. Exhausted, I went in the bus station, made a phone call, and arranged my partner at the time to get me a ticket home, seeing how I literally only had what I was wearing and my DD2-14 with me.

I looked like a terrorist with no luggage. I was in desperate need of some physical hygiene. I was mortified. All eyes were focused on me. Degrading comments people said as they walked by, "You smell, loser, blah, blah, blah." At least I was on my way home.

Finally, as I board the bus, my anxiety levels take a nosedive down to the relatively calm state. It would be just pure exhaustion, yet I am not tired in the least bit. I don't know how. In fact, I am running on pure adrenaline. I can't wait to get off this bus and get back into some normalcy. The bus is filling up quickly. I watch a variety of different people board. I find it comforting seeing the non-uniformed people.

Chapter Nineteen

After what seemed to be weeks on that bus home, we finally arrived at our final destination. Everyone is exiting the bus and gathering their belongings. Then there is me, I just need to walk off. No luggage but so much baggage. What was I coming home to?

What was going to happen between me and William and our children? Were these diagnoses really going to have lasting impact in my life? What was Lozano going to do now that she couldn't send "care packages" in my name to the ship? What is going to happen now that I know about how the heroin comes in and goes out?

My head is a swirling mess. I haven't been given anything, so I am on edge. I feel so sick to my stomach. I think this is the start of withdrawal feels like. At least I'm in my home state of Arizona. I can make it to the house from the bus station. I already made it this far.

I collect call my house to find that no one answered. I walked home to find my house was empty. There were no signs of my children being here. William and all our children's belongings were gone. I searched every room; they all indicate the worst, that William had taken our children and left.

Hours have passed, and still William did not show up. Where did he go? It must have been 0200 when a set of headlights pulled into the driveway. I ran to the door to see if William and the kids were home. To my surprise, it was my red Infinity that pulled in, but it was not William who got out.

"Lozano!" Even when you are out, you are not truly out. Lozano and her heroin-smuggling family remained in my life for several years to come. Just like that, I was free from the military but imprisoned to a different militia.

Chapter Twenty

I let my baggage consume me. I was stuffed inside a luggage bag like an item. There is no one to blame for keeping me locked inside of this luggage. I could be freed from this heroin addiction, MST, PTSD, Anxiety, Depression, Agoraphobia, Aids and Schizophrenia as soon as I wanted to. I was the key to open the luggage that I carry, but yet, I had the mentality of thinking I was stuck in the luggage.

I just wanted to give up so many times. I couldn't even give up because that would mean I tried and failed. You see, I didn't even try, I just wept and tried to answer myself. Why did these injustices happen to me, what did I do to deserve them?

How can anyone ask how I caused the rapes, human smuggling, and drug addiction that were bestowed upon me? Anyone would say, "No, of course you did not deserve those things to happen to you, those people are not human, they will be paid back." I agreed. I took on the victim mindset and adopted it as mine. That was the wrong move and that thought kept me as my own prisoner.

It is not easy to switch your way of thinking. How can you just flip a switch and have a different mindset? That has to be an adjustment, a difficult one, too. I can share with you all who want to hear. It was difficult, so difficult that I am shocked to be alive today. It nearly took my life in order for me to see that I even had a life to take.

Chapter Twenty-One

Years after being released from the military, I was still in the claws of a different militia. I was smuggled out of the military and into the cartel. The Lozano family were the ones who I was involved with. Ursula Lozano was the shipmate that brought me comfort and my newfound addiction. I believed at the time I was being taken care of by her in the sense that if I wasn't with her, those terrible awful things wouldn't happen. Now the terrible things that could happen, she told me she was saving me from. I believed if she was happy, I was safe. Safe from what you ask? I'll tell you what, from her brother. Her brother was a boss in the cartel. He is a very violent man.

He is charming and seems to be an upstanding citizen. He is in charge of a well-known and established air conditioning company. Down south in Laredo Texas, you and everyone else need an air conditioning unit. He goes to work every day. He never gets his hands dirty, yet he has his hands in everything.

This family hires immigrant women to be their house maids. They pay them in cash and gain their trust. While the women are kept here illegally, they have children who are born here in America so their children have citizenship. The illegal women stay silence in the hopes they do not get found and deported, having to leave their children or be forced to take them away from everything they know.

Where are the men? Where are the protectors? These men are just as easily recruited; not only are they controlled with an addiction, knowingly or not, but they are also forced to go back and forth between Mexico and America and perform whatever task was said to be carried out. If the men do not do as they are told, then they are threatened with their women and children just on the other side of the border.

So when Juan gives the order to murder someone, the order stands as you do it or your wife and children die. Or the order that you deliver goods for cash and return the cash to him, of course, causing these men now to become felons. Juan has got them all now. He is in control, still while being that upstanding citizen.

He is sex trafficking the teenage girls and young adults to do anything he desires you to do. You have a choice, you do what you are told, or you don't get fed or a place to sleep. These girls and young women are controlled with addictions and threats.

One of the most awful things I saw was that Juan had his house maid sign over custody to a member in his family in case the mother was to get deported. Juan could have her deported at any moment with just a call. But as long as she does what he tells her, there is nothing to worry about.

Chapter Twenty-Two

The Lozano family smuggled heroin from Mexico to America. They used the United States Navy to smuggle in and out both people and drugs. Once they had their shitbag kicked out of the military, they could now suck them dry. And I do mean dry.

I was paying the rent each month for myself and Ursula. She never helped, in fact she would take the money and spend it on drugs. If I couldn't come up with the money to recover what she took, we would be removed from our apartment. She would go to work each night, but never did she get paid. It was always she had to get something out to pawn or she had to give Juan money.

Ursula didn't care if she got kicked out of the apartment, because she had somewhere else to go, someone else to pay for her. I was alone. I literally didn't have one person down there. Seeing how William took the kids and threatened my life, I had no one, just me, just Ursula. My luggage that just kept getting heavier and heavier.

The months were getting so hard. I couldn't keep making the rent twice a month plus be able to eat. It was one or the other and more times than I would like to admit, eating was the last thing of importance.

I didn't make much. The negative DD2-14 held me back from getting any job. The fact that I do not speak Spanish was a challenge all on its own. No one in Laredo wanted to hire a Yankee, let alone one that they said they needed to wear sunglasses to look at.

I sold the living room set, all my jewelry, electronics. I even sold my respect and started working as a topless dancer just to be able to keep up with the demands. Ursula did that, too, and she told me if her brother found out that she was doing this, he would kill me and her. But what choice did I have? I had to keep a roof over our heads.

Ursula continued to tell Juan that she worked at the immigration center; that's where he told her to work. She did work there, but she blew it off most nights. I don't know how she held that job with all her missed days, but she did.

Chapter Twenty-Three

One night, she blew work off again, and it was a night I didn't go to the truck stop to work. Two men came to the back window of the apartment and were breaking in! I saw the shadows of them come up to the bedroom window, which was the only window. They used a knife to cut the screen. Their shadows were reflecting off the wall and the mirror. The rims of their hats hid their faces. They were dressed in dark hoodies and jeans, and I couldn't see their faces.

Who are these men? Why are they breaking and entering? I do not have anything worth value! What are they planning on doing to us? God help us, I prayed. I was supposed to be home alone, as far as Juan knew. Ursula was not supposed to be home.

The two men broke open the back window as I laid there in bed. I was so afraid for my life. Flashbacks of what Agular did while on the ship flashed before my eyes. I was petrified; I couldn't move, I could barely speak. Ursula immediately jumped into action and grabbed a kitchen knife and sliced one of their arms open and yelled something in Spanish. I'm sure it wasn't friendly. The men fled. She just saved me from something terrible that those men had in mind.

Ursula and I were okay. But I was so afraid that I begged her to call her mother and ask if we could just stay there for the night. I was not able to calm down enough to stay. To my surprise, when Ursula called her mother, her conversation was half in Spanish and half in English. I was able to pick up some of it.

Ursula was begging her mother to please let us stay. Her mother did not say yes; instead, she called Juan and told him Ursula wasn't at work. Her mother yelled at Ursula, telling her repeatedly, "You weren't supposed to be home."

Ursula then got a call from Juan demanding to know why she missed work! She was not supposed to be home. Those men where there for me and not her. I am glad she was there. I could only imagine what they would have done to me. I did not sleep for long after that. It was like I was too afraid to sleep, so I would take naps, not really sleeping.

I was on edge all the time after this. Everyone was suspect, even Ursula. Did she have something to do with this? At the very moment, I would have said no. But hindsight is so powerful.

No one wants to believe the horror stories or what is right in front of them. They like to think they know best, but no one else really knows. Well, I can say I definitely was thinking like this. My mind was malfunctioning. I could not process anything, it was as if I was shut off, coasting on auto pilot. Now I know that it wasn't a fault, it was a reaction to me being held hostage, resulting in Stockholm syndrome.

I really wish I knew than what I know now. I could have saved myself years of anguish and utter destruction. I guess that is the power in hindsight in full action. Now that I can see clearer and my mind is not malfunctioning as it once was, I see the truth. I see that I was in a hostage situation, I was a captive with no visible restraints.

Chapter Twenty- Four

The situation became distressing. I thought of topless dancing as the most undignified action I could do. But then, we had to come up with more money because apparently the rent that was said to have been paid was in fact not paid. I refused to strip more over this. I didn't want to be stripping in the first place. It was humiliating.

Then, Ursula wanted for us to start making sexually explicit websites to make money. I was not down for this either. It resulted in the scar that runs across my bottom lip to this day. Yes, that's right, wham! I was punched in the face a few times to teach me a lesson. Ursula just punched me in the face!

Even in hindsight, I do not know what kept me from fighting her back. I just thought that she did not get any love or at least not enough love as a child, seeing as that her dad died from a heroin addiction well she was so young. Never did I think that she was suffering from any mental illnesses. Looking back, I think she suffered from several mental illnesses.

With my busted-up face, I put a hindrance on our money coming in. Ursula reached out to Juan, and he sent for us to come and see him in San Antonio. He saw my face and took

Ursula out back for forty-five minutes or so, leaving me sit inside his lovely home while I waited.

When Ursula came in, she and Juan only spoke Spanish, no English at all, so I barely understood them. She and I left his home and went to Laredo. I asked how he was planning on helping us. Ursula told me that she just had to convince him not to kill me! He had every intention of shooting me and leaving me dead on some ranch. What? I cannot believe what she is saying to me. He wanted me dead! How, then, am I still alive? Really, how the hell am I still alive? By the grace of God.

I asked her. "What did you say to him? Why does he want me dead? What about my children?" My panic was in a full-blown fury. Ursula pulled over to a motel and got a room. My questioning and panic were too overwhelming for her. I didn't want to get out of the car, and we fought over me getting out. I thought I was going to be killed right there in that motel.

Once we settled down some, she explained he was not going to kill me after all. She was trying to tell me something but was holding back. I kept insisting that she told me, that me knowing was the only thing that could calm me down. "Please, just tell me."

Ursula then said, "He's not going to kill you, Betty; he's going to go after your children." I never told a soul that before now. I was in pure shock. I can't bear to even think about even threatening a person's child. Ursula continued to tell me that as long as we pay him back for me missing a week or two worth of work, he would leave my children alone.

Apparently, he gave her money for a motel, food, and a month's worth of rent. She did not use the money to pay our rent, so now we were living in a car, breaking into her mother's house to shower after she went to work. Ursula would always take a tool or something to pawn for even more money, telling me we had to pay it back. We just kept getting deeper and deeper.

Chapter Twenty-Five

Ursula always had her smoke without fail. If she wasn't able to smoke, she would literally turn into the devil herself. The rage that came out of her was terrifying. She would smash anything in her sight! Her pupils would dilate so much that there was just blackness staring at you. She would con the elderly into giving her cash if she gave them a ride to work from someone's house. It seems as if it was only old ladies that needed a ride.

I was made to stay in this apartment of her friend while she took the ladies to work. This place, which she told me was her friend's house, was the worst place I have ever been to in my life! I think it was hell.

There were giant cockroaches crawling about. There were dishes and filth and so much stuff. This place was stuffed with trash. I wanted to just set it on fire. But there was a child who lived there all day and night alone and in the midst of all this trash was a queen-sized bed. It was made, but garbage and trash surrounded it. There was nothing to clean with. This poor child, she had it so bad. I wanted to call Child Protective Services, but I had no phone. I had to sell mine to get some money.

Ursula said this is normal housing in Laredo and that I was being a princess for thinking it was not enough. There was room on one stove top burner to cook an egg for the child if she needed to eat. There was Kool-Aid in the refrigerator. There wasn't any soap in the bathroom. Soap would not have been enough.

I don't know whatever happened with that child. We stayed there for a couple of days before I got a hold of a phone and reported the situation to CPS for help. We ended up leaving there and going to her mother's house where I fell ill. Ursula kept telling me I was sick because I would not eat. You can't eat when there is nothing to eat. I lost a significant amount of weight while here.

I was on to them. They had been lacing my food and cigarettes with heroin, keeping me addicted to her. Keeping me a prisoner. I broke free. I told Ursula that my brother had been in ICU and was given his last rights. I told her I had to fly home. I am not going to tell you all the horrible things that have taken place to get to the point where I was allowed to fly home. I will just tell you how I broke free.

Chapter Twenty-Six

When I broke away physically, that isn't what freed me. I was still mentally captive to the massacres I had been through. I needed to be saved from the strongholds that had captured my mind and soul. I don't know how one can recover their soul once they feel it has been shattered, but there is a way, and I found it!

I had to center my life on Jesus and allow him to take the wheel because I had lost control. I had to let go of everything that was me up until that point. I needed to be made new. I set out on a spiritual conquest to rectify my inner spirit. This is a tool for anyone to grab hold of and use for their own needs. It just takes determination, declaration, and hunger.

You personally have to make the choice, and the rest will take place. I made the choice; I wanted my life to be different. I wanted all of the strongholds to be gone from me. I did not want to be afraid and silenced anymore. I wanted to live.

When I made my decision to live, it was as if I felt the breath of God inside of me. I accepted that Jesus was in control, and everything about me was changed for the good with those words alone! Jesus is my rescuer and died for me and you to be saved, forgiven, and made new.

Chapter Twenty-Seven

Weeks, months, and even years passed. I kept the faith. I kept praying and devoting my time and energies to the Lord our God. I noticed things in my life change. I was changing. I was changing with such grace and beauty. The strongholds that were once death sentences are now my life sentences. Relationships that would have been considered hopeless are back to life and vibrant.

My daughter went over a decade without speaking to me or even seeing me. She was doing everything in her power to keep me out of her life. She has begun to let me in. I hear the naysayers say she grew up, that's why she came around. But that isn't it. How many adults do we know that make a decision to keep someone out and let them back in? Not many. Most adults hold grudges for the length of or damn near all their lives. So, for my daughter to come around on her own, I owe it all to the power of prayer.

I never stopped praying for her to one day come back to me. God had plans for us. He used that time apart to mold me into the person that I need to be for my daughter. As harsh as that seems, that period of growing was for the best. I was able to grow and change, and she was able to grow and change.

Today, she and I have a relationship that is still tender. Nonetheless, it is a relationship that will never be finished. She is my lifelong friend.

She and I started a non-profit group to help teenagers and their parents get through hard time, and to help assure them they are loved and that there are better days ahead of them. A parent's bond is something that cannot be easily broken. Even when you think it is beyond repair, there is hope. She and I tell all who listen about the hardships of our relationship in hopes to plant the seed of repair for someone else.

I know it was hard for my daughter to see her mother fight through her mental illnesses, but it was worth it. Not only did she see me fight them, but she also saw and helped me defeat them. Bean is in pursuit of becoming a registered nurse to specialize in mental health. And for me, I am in pursuit to share how I broke free.

I tried all the therapy I could and learned a lot, but that is not what actually cured me. I was cured by the grace of God through Jesus. I prayed and prayed; even in the darkest of times, I prayed. The more I prayed, the more my steps landed me in the right place at the right time. I could feel the overwhelming power that was happening around me directing me in God's direction.

Chapter Twenty-Eight

My depression melted off. Sure, the situations that caused me depression are sad and depressing, but something was different now. I had a new sense of strength, security, peace. Now I wasn't suffering from depression I was controlling my depression. My brokenness is what has rebuilt me stronger, more humble, wiser. Everything that was there that seemed as if it were going to be the death of me, was actually the rebirth of me. That destruction was necessary for my rebirth into the beautiful woman that is free from the depression! All because it is God's will for me and all of us to be freed.

I still have bouts of anxiety that quickly floods me, but just as fast as that anxiety floods me, I am washed free from the anxiety. As quick as it comes in, it is just as quick on its way out. Anxiety does not have a hold over me. God restored me. He has given me peace over my anxiety.

I surrendered my life over to God. I could see and feel the outstretched hand of God guiding me through it all. I took that anxiety and was granted the ability to use it for good. I learned a way to deal with the anxiety, so that I may share my insight with others. I lead support meetings for those trying to overcome their own anxieties.

After nearly two decades my DD 2-14 was reconsidered and changed to an honorable discharge. They had gathered all the information that they needed to prove the first one was a mistake. I didn't even know the federal government was still working on this.

This was a blessing, a miracle at the finest! This was perfect timing. This was God's timing. This is a moment and a decision that opened more opportunities for me that I could have imagined. I was comforted beyond belief. Doors from multiple businesses opened their door of employment for me.

I haven't heard from the Lozano family in decades. You are probably asking yourself; how can I live so peacefully not knowing if someone is after my family. But I ask you, with God how can you not?

God doesn't take away aids, or does he? Yes, he does. I went two decades with not knowing for sure, if in fact I had aids. I just went on the fact that since I was sexually assaulted, I had to be safe to assume I was infected. A dear family friend of mine was in need of a kidney; she had a rare blood type and only one percent of people will actually match her.

When I found out that she was in need my fear and anxieties was silenced in their tracks and God's voice came out of me and I offered to be tested to help her. I was not sure if I was even the correct blood type, let alone safe to donate an organ. My entire life I told myself I would never donate an organ; They were inside of me, so therefore they are mine. Yet there I stood having just offered my kidney!

I cannot believe I offered, that's why I say it was the voice of God speaking through me. After going through a series of testing not only was I a perfect match to Mariam's blood type, I was of the one percent who she needed to be paired with.

I also found out that I was, in fact, negative for AIDS. All those years living prisoner to my fears, vanished. Mariam's need was my strength to finally get tested and how great it was to know the truth. I thank God every day that I had the spare part that helps keep Mariam alive and well today.

Yes, Jesus does free us from all things, including ourselves. I find that I have to stay healthy, so I have to go for walks. Which are outside and getting me out and about in the community. Taking me places I spent years avoiding, gone.

My fear actually turned out to be my strength. Mariam's organ failure fright became a working delight. I am truly thankful that I could help another person in need on such a Godly level.

Chapter Twenty-Nine

You know the saying, "My life just flashed before my eyes?" Good. That just happened to me. It was as fast as the speed of light, my life was revealed to me, right there in my cozy living room, with the "Golden Girls" playing in the background. Days after the surgery, there I was, writing my story to share with all of you who will read it or listen.

The Golden Girls were on when I was a little girl at my grandmother's house, and I would wonder what I would do with the rest of my life. I remember when one of the girl's friends said she wrote a book; at that moment, I thought that is what I wanted to do. So innocently I thought about how I would be when I was an adult writer, not considering any negatives or no's along the way, just pure, peaceful daydreaming. Forty plus years later, here I am, an adult writer. God has been right with me every step of my way, even in the negatives and all the no's.

God is so good all the time. Jesus takes what the enemy meant for evil and turns it for good. Never give up, because at any moment it will be revealed to you- your path that God has for you.

All those years wasted thinking I had AIDS, I did not see as wasted. No, I see it as a purpose, my purpose to share my journey with God to go and disciple him to others. And that's what I do. I find and meet new disciples everywhere I go.

I find that my passion stems for my love of Jesus. He is who gets me through, and he's willing to forgive me. He will do that same for you, too. We all are given that gift. I pray that every person comes to know and love the Lord. He is my rescue story. He is my life story.

Chapter Thirty

I encourage all people, myself included, to search for Jesus in all that we do. Find a church that you can call your home of worship, your church. Base your life with Jesus front and center. Everything else will just be revealed at the perfect timing, God's timing. It is this hope that continually gets me through this life! It is the holy spirit that carries me wherever I go. Our lives are so precious from the start, even when life gets you to think that your life isn't. That is, when your faith and hope are revealed to God. Pour out your hearts to Jesus, and he will reign in forgiveness and love that will repair and teach us what and wherever our journeys bring us for eternity.

It is the revival that my spirit loves and needs to thrive. I encourage you to make it yours along with me. It's hard for me to put into words the transformation I went through from being a human smuggled to this point today. It is just as difficult as it is to find the right words; it is just as easy to be set free from it.

Once you let go and let God, there is no stopping it. We are in God's hands. This is my rescue story.

Dedication

"Thank you to our Lord Almighty God, through his son,
our savior Jesus.

May peace be with us all."